The Book of Haipoos

The Book of Haipoos

Written by Bronwyn Whittle
Poem illustrations by Jens Ranieri

That was too much bread.

"Is there such a thing", I asked?

"Yes", my butthole said.

Oh Diarrhea,

I long to live without ya,

AH! MOVE! GOTTA GO!

Mom, I am concerned.

Is it bad if a lil poop

Went back up my butt?

"FODMAP"

Onions and garlic

Will set the vampires running,

And my poo-poo too.

Coffee anyone?

Just one moment on the lips,

An hour with the shits.

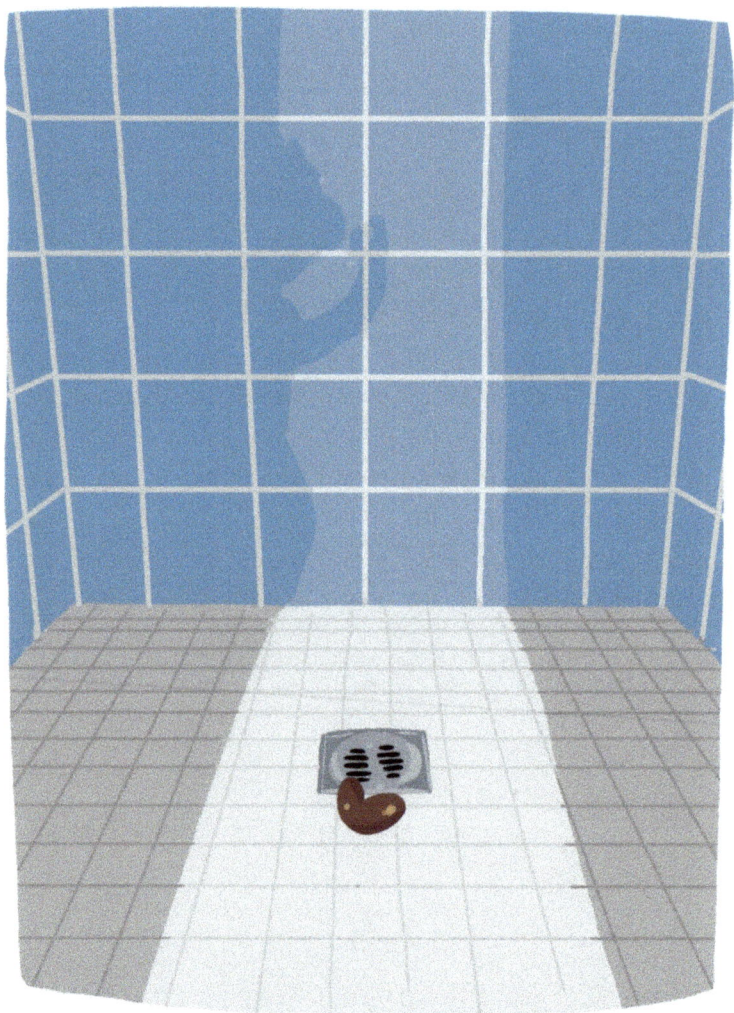

In the darkest hour,

In a college shower, lies

A mystery poo.

Is it called fast food

Because of the rapid speed

It exits my butt?

It doesn't take much

To awaken and shake him.

The ol' butthole troll.

"I'll just wait to poo",

I said to myself today.

We make plans, butts laugh.

"I beg your pardon,

I do hate to interrupt."

Said my poops NEVER

I sat on the loo.

Push, squeeze, heave, hulla-baloo.

Nope, no poo for you.

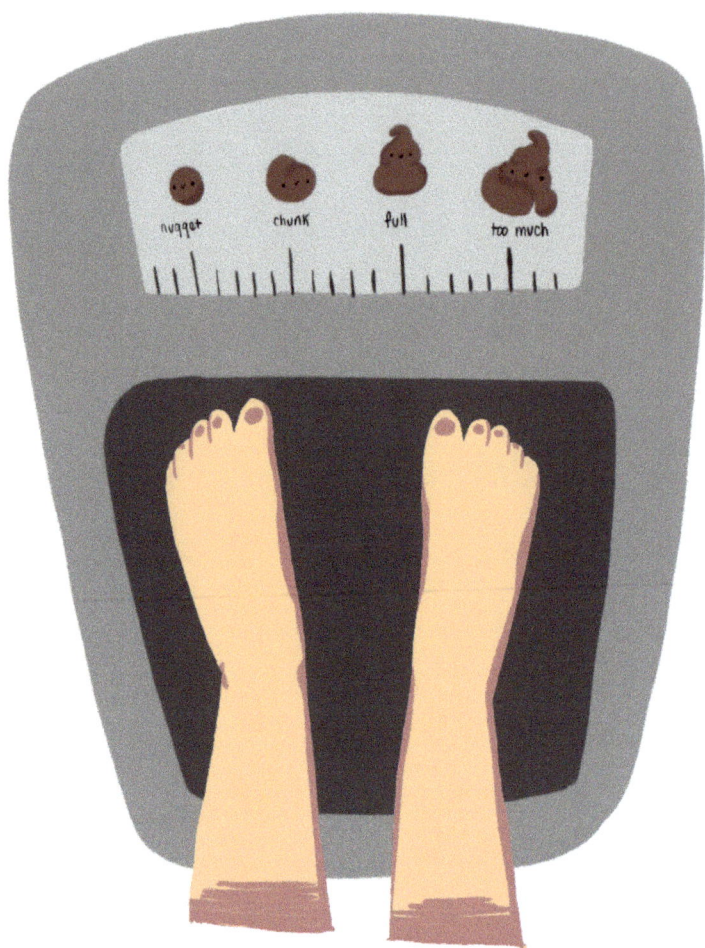

I don't understand

How I shit this much each day,

And still weigh this much.

I felt the pressure,

So I pushed. Thought it was farts,

Now... I fart in fear.

Am I successful?

Today my poop was solid,

So yes. Yes, very.

Thanks to McDonald's

I finally understand

The phrase "a shit ton".

I feel it happen,

But when I look down... nothing.

The Phantom Poop. Boo.

Sometimes it takes hours,

Sometimes it's done in a flash.

Never a dull poo.

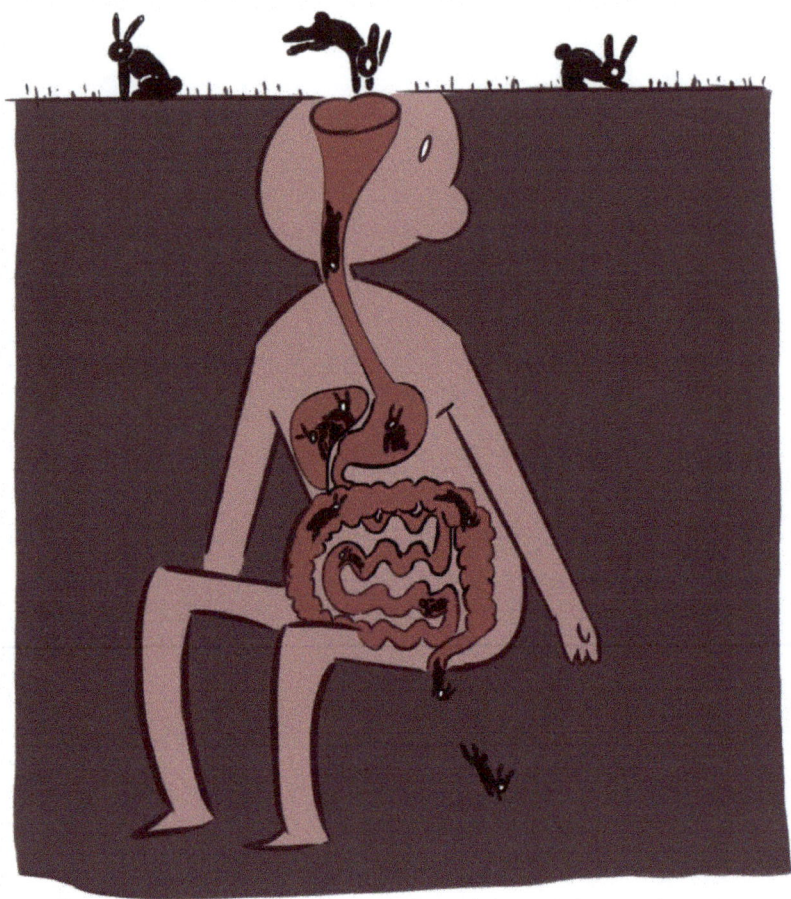

"Easter"

Chocolate bunnies.

Bite and chew, swallow and wait

For them to escape.

The subway rolls on.

I pray, while counting the stops,

That my butt won't pop.

poopmaster >

iMessage
Today 4:20 PM

> What to do, to do,
> With all this unwanted poo?
> I'll live in a zoo!

It's stinky, stinky,
To poop all the time, ya know?
Hmmm, when will it stop?

> Hmmm, maybe never?
> Maybe it's this forever?
> Just shoot me, okay?

I will not shoot you!
One day you will stop pooping.
Sooner the better

Popped a blood vessel.

Pooping can get dangerous,

When push comes to shove.

He's in and he's out,

Turtling all about, that poo.

Who knows what he'll do.

"Greetings"

Oh wow Cynthia,

What a lovely home you have,

Where is the toilet?

'Beans Beans' by Bronwyn Whittle

The magical fruit,
the more you eat, the more you ~~toot~~ shit yourself senseless

Who are these people

That can just hold their poop in?

Who are these wizards?!

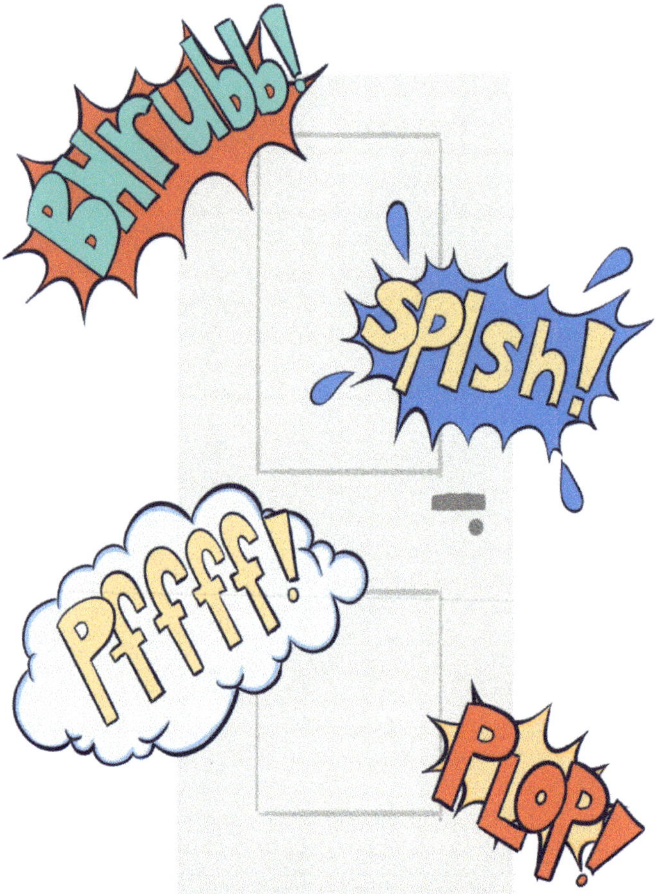
BHrubb!
SPlsh!
Pffff!
PLOP!

"Onomatopoeia"

BHrubb fffigggplob polb polb,

SSsss nngeeefuh splsh pilpilbb pss,

Pfffff plob plop plop pip.

I think orchestras

Could use a new wind section.

A chorus of butts.

The fart emerges

From the winter coat cocoon.

Fly, Flutterfart, fly.

I feel a bubble

In the rubble and I know

There will be trouble.

Each fart represents

The food that came before it.

Respect the food ghosts.

Harsh, hotheaded poops.

It sounds like my own butthole

Is cursing me out.

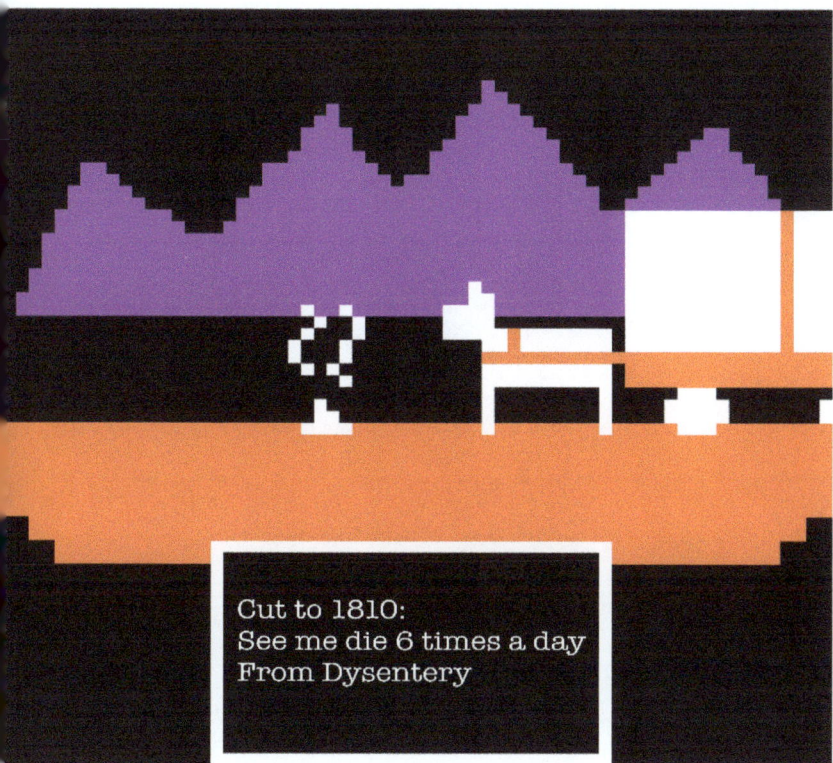

Cut to 1810:
See me die 6 times a day
From Dysentery

"A Prayer"

Do not poop your pants.

Close eyes. Breathe deep. Run to loo.

Do not. Poop. Your. Pants.

Strutting and farting,

Leaving a trail of stinky

For the catcallers.

Date somebody? Why?!

Holding in farts all the time?

Not the life for me.

A cappella groups!

Anyone need a beat box?

My butt is ready.

All these pulsations

Revving in my gas station,

Pipes are gonna burst!

Empty Subway car

Rolling into the station.

Someone must have pooped.

Sometimes I think, "Oh,

Is that a didgeridoo?"

But it's just my fart.

Why would anyone

Pay money for laxatives?

Just eat burritos!

Silent, toxic, warm.

Traits of a fart that warns of

Impending shitstorms.

A fart is to poo,

As thunder is to lightning.

My SAT prep.

So disheartening

To still be sharting myself

As a grown adult.

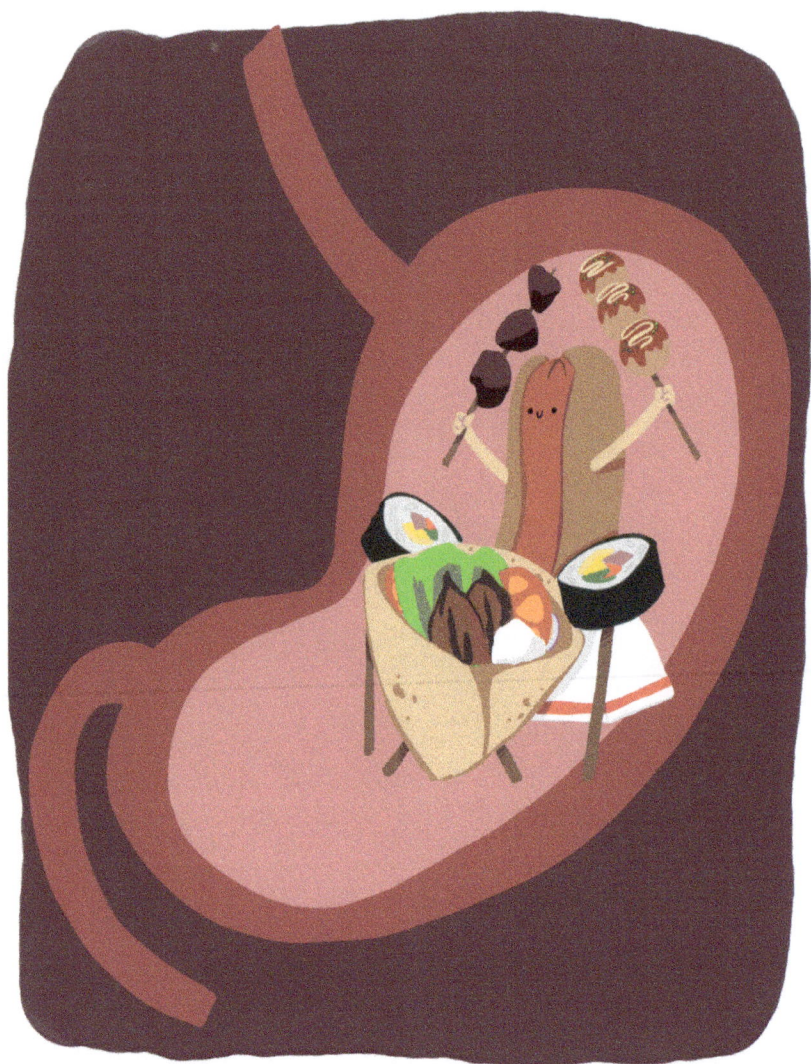

When the street meat treat,

Haunts your belly with a beat...

Pray, and move your feet.

Ok! We can date.

But I fart all of the time.

Hope you're into that.

I see but his head,
My sewer snake. And who knows
Just how far he goes.

"Party Pooper"

We all have that friend

Who poops on the bathroom floor

At parties. Wait, right?

"The Penguin Walk of Shame"

Waddle and waddle,

With poop between your butt cheeks.

Hope your pants don't leak!

Endlessly impressed,

By the symphony of sound

Produced by my butt.

My superpower?

Constipation AND the runs,

All in one sitting.

I'll have one burger,

Milkshake, fries, chicken strips and

Toilet directions.

And in local news:

Garlic induced poop attack

Ruins girls love life.

Tikka stained fingers,

And curry stained toilet bowl.

But still no regrets.

Babies do it. Cute.

But when I poop my pants? NooooOooo.

"I have a problem"

You know the saying?

When life hands you runny poo,

Write a good haiku!

Guest Bathroom

Attention:

The following poems were donated
by guest poets, or Pooets as I like to
say. This wonderful group of Pooets
consists of friends and family members
Who had such powerful poop stories of
their own that they had to share.

Enjoy, and remember to wash your hands!

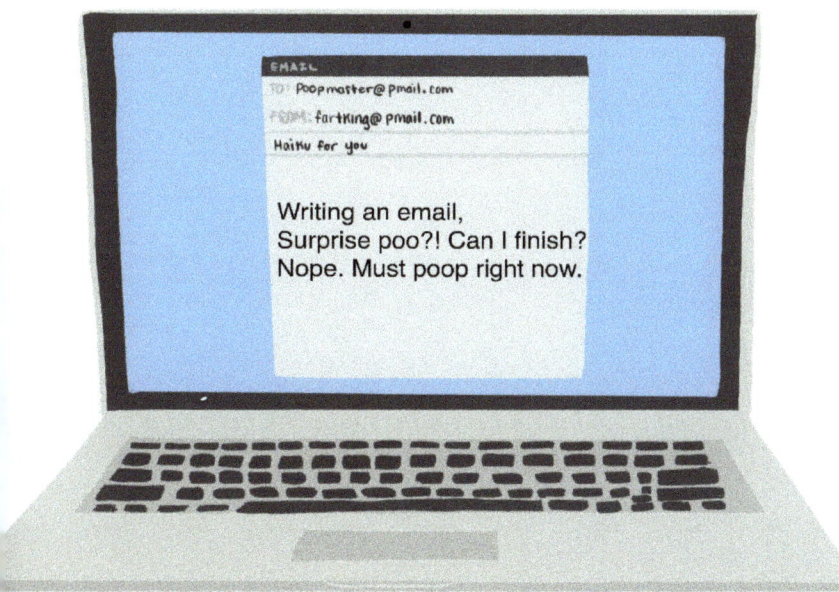

EMAIL

TO: poopmaster@pmail.com

FROM: fartking@pmail.com

Haiku for you

Writing an email,
Surprise poo?! Can I finish?
Nope. Must poop right now.

By Julia Karis

Spent the hours pushing.

YES! A Satisfying plop.

A glance down....not much.

By Kelly Hubbell

Drank the whole night through,

Hangover is here today,

Rough poop on the way!

By Julia Karis

The throne awaits me.

Take me to pure ecstasy,

Butthole Chariot.

By Lorenzo Preston

I pushed out my poop

For so long, it must be huge!

It's a pebble...how.

By *Julia Karis*

Chicken and waffles

I love you dearly, so please,

Dont make my butt pee.

By Nicholas Hawks

"Smothered"

Smothered burrito,

Feel it build from head to toe,

Butt bleeding queso.

By Lorenzo Preston

Traveling is fun,

But new places can bring nerves,

No pooping occurs.

By Julia Karis

"Open Late"

Drop the Chalupa

Just like cheesy beans and rice

It moves right through ya.

By Lorenzo Preston

"Vindaloo Loo Loo"

Chicken Vindaloo.

Just as hot, even as poo.

Loo. Loo! Where's the loo!?

By Nicholas Hawks

Gave new food a try.

That Korean BBQ?

Keep a toilet near.

By Julia Karis

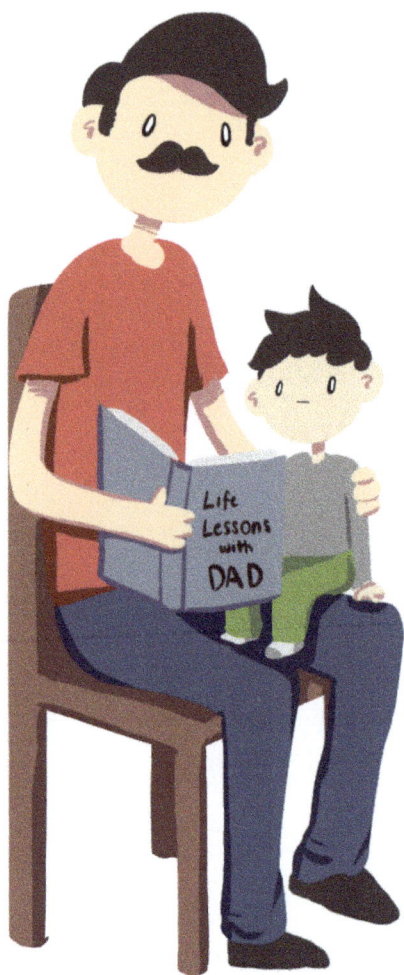

"Truer Words"

Son? Yes? Some advice:

Take good care of your asshole.

Seriously though.

By Nicholas Hawks

Let's talk about poo.

It's something we all do do,

Mostly on the loo.

By Grace Whittle

"Butt-trayal"

Pants around my feet

Poop between my cheeks- but wait!

Betrayed!! No TP!

By Nicholas Hawks

The candles were blown

Cake consumed and in the can

Surprise continued.

By Alyssa Florio

DEUCES

www.ingramcontent.com/pod-product-compliance
Lightning Source LLC
Chambersburg PA
CBHW041823090426
42811CB00010B/1095